KEEP START STOP DELIVER

Prayer
Companion

Todd Crippin

Keep, Start, Stop, and Deliver: Prayer Companion
Todd Crippin
Published by JMH Publishing, Overland Park, Kansas

Copyright ©2024 Todd Crippin
All rights reserved.

Unless otherwise indicated, all Scripture quotations are from The ESV® Bible (The Holy Bible, English Standard Version®), © 2001 by Crossway, a publishing ministry of Good News Publishers. Used by permission. All rights reserved.

Scripture quotations marked (GNT) are from the Good News Translation in Today's English Version-Second Edition. Copyright © 1992 by American Bible Society. Used by Permission.

Scripture quotations marked (NIV) are taken from the Holy Bible, New International Version®, NIV®. Copyright © 1973, 1978, 1984, 2011 by Biblica, Inc.™ Used by permission of Zondervan. All rights reserved worldwide. www.zondervan.com. The "NIV" and "New International Version" are trademarks registered in the United States Patent and Trademark Office by Biblica, Inc.™

Scripture quotations marked (AMP) are taken from the Amplified Bible, Copyright © 2015 by The Lockman Foundation. Used by permission.

Project Management and Book Design: Davis Creative Publishing, DavisCreativePublishing.com
Editor: Kimberly Fletcher

Library of Congress Cataloging-in-Publication Data
Library of Congress Control Number: 2024922866
Todd Crippin
Keep, Start, Stop, Deliver: Prayer Companion
ISBN: 979-8-9906241-1-5 (paperback) | 979-8-9906241-2-2 (ebook)
Library of Congress subject headings: REL022000 RELIGION / Devotional
2024

ATTENTION CORPORATIONS, UNIVERSITIES, COLLEGES, AND PROFESSIONAL ORGANIZATIONS: Quantity discounts are available on bulk purchases of this book for educational, gift purposes, or as premiums for increasing magazine subscriptions or renewals. Special books or book excerpts can also be created to fit specific needs. For information, please contact JMH Publishing, td.crippin@gmail.com

For Kent and Christine

To my mother, Christine, the most devoted prayer warrior I've ever known. And to my father, Kent, who always reminded us of the power of prayer. I love and miss you both.

We are glad you have picked up the
Keep, Start, Stop, and Deliver:
Prayer Companion!

If you would like to read the original book
that inspired the one you are holding,
Keep, Start, Stop, and Deliver:
An Active Devotional,
please order your copy at
www.activedevotional.com.

You can connect with Todd by
scanning this QR code with
the camera on your smartphone.

INTRODUCTION

Prayer is a strong form of communication with God and such a privilege. Throughout the Bible, we read and see the impact of powerful prayers and are told to pray without ceasing. We can express ourselves fully to God when we fellowship with him. We may ask him to take control of a difficult situation, give adoration to him, or confess our sins. Whatever our prayer may be, know that the God of the universe delights in our willingness to spend time with him.

As I have journeyed through my first book, *Keep, Start, Stop, Deliver: An Active Devotional*, I found myself not praying about my statements and my discernment of the Scripture. I know the importance of praying Scripture as we memorize it. With this understanding, it became clear that for all its benefits, the devotional still needed an even greater emphasis on prayer.

To fill this hole, I created what you are holding in your hands—a simple but powerful prayer companion. You'll find a prayer on each page that directly ties to the weekly Scripture from the devotional. These are my personal prayers that came to me when I meditated on the Bible verses and reflected on my responses to my *Keep, Start, Stop, Deliver* statements.

I hope this prayer companion inspires you to develop your own prayers. Take the time to write them down. You can use my prayers as a template or create your own based on the Scripture and reflection for a particular week.

No matter your approach, never doubt that your words are not good enough for God or that he doesn't listen. He does listen, and he longs to hear from you. If you are unsure, look to the Psalms written by David. David was never ashamed to cry out to God in times of distress or great joy. Let his life inspire you. Remember, God doesn't just want to hear you pray; he wants you to listen, too. He listens to you, so take time to listen to him. He is waiting to talk with you, to commune with you. Begin praying today.

You can find me on Facebook and Instagram under ActiveDevotional. If you are willing to share insights you receive from this book—be it praises, concerns, or general thoughts—I want to hear from you. You can reach me at activedevotional@gmail.com. My website, www.activedevotional.com, also allows you to watch my videos, stay updated on upcoming books and events, and talk with me about your spiritual journey.

Thank you for your purchase. I hope we grow in God's love for him and for each other. Now...

Keep, Start, Stop, and *Deliver*, and feel the power of prayer.

Week 1

And let us consider how to stir up one another to love and good works.
Hebrews 10:24

Lord, open my heart so I may understand how you want me to act and speak to my brothers and sisters in Christ as well as to those who do not yet know you. Let my actions spur them to action, and my love for you draw them closer. Let me consider every thought, word, and action before I speak or act and its impact on your mission. In Christ's name, I pray. Amen!

Week 2

■ ■ ■

For God gave us a spirit not of fear but of power and love and self-control.
2 Timothy 1:7

Jesus, regardless of my circumstances on any given day or even any given minute, let me find strength in you. Rise up Spirit within me to clear the anxiety and distress from my soul. Allow me the room to grow and mature in your ways. Holy Spirit, allow me to understand your power, your love, and the self-control my Savior, Jesus, had so that while he was tempted, he never sinned. I pray these things in your sweet name, Jesus. Amen!

Week 3

Therefore, confess your sins to one another and pray for one another, that you may be healed. The prayer of a righteous person has great power as it is working.
James 5:16

Father, allow me to understand the power of prayer. Let me recall the faith of the friends who lowered the mat on which their paralytic friend laid. They lowered him through the roof, knowing Jesus would heal their friend. Let me build trust with another Christ follower. Permit me to be transparent to this person about my sinful nature so that together we can raise our sins to you and feel your loving forgiveness as only you can truly forgive and restore in me a faith that is indescribable. In your name, I pray. Amen!

Week 4

■ ■ ■

Blessed be the God and Father of our Lord Jesus Christ, the Father of mercies and God of all comfort, who comforts us in all our affliction, so that we may be able to comfort those who are in any affliction, with the comfort with which we ourselves are comforted by God.
2 Corinthians 1:3-4

Lord, I can be angry, lonely, depressed, anxious, and happy all within a simple minute, it seems at times. Please give me comfort from my emotions, for they are fleeting, but your presence is never-ending. May the afflictions I struggle with, be they physical, emotional, or spiritual, be healed by you in a way that I can comprehend. Let the purpose behind your restoration be apparent so I may comfort others in their afflictions as you lead me. Thank you, Jesus. Amen!

Week 5

Be obedient to God, and do not allow your lives to be shaped by those desires you had when you were still ignorant.
Instead, be holy in all that you do, just as God who called you is holy.
1 Peter 1:14-15 (GNT)

Holy Father, I thank you for your grace and mercy that you give freely to me. As I reflect upon your sacrifice Jesus, let me be obedient to your commands. Let me love you, God, with all my heart, soul, and mind while I also love others as you love me. I ask that you guard my heart so I do not focus on the desires of this world but cast my gaze upon your kingdom. Give me the wisdom to understand the difference. In your name, I pray. Amen!

Week 6

*And let the peace of Christ rule in your
hearts, to which indeed you were called in
one body. And be thankful.
Colossians 3:15*

I thank you, God, for everything you have given me.
Thank you for allowing me to be content but not
complacent; to be alone with you but not isolated
from others; to experience your joyful blessings and
the blessings that come from tears; to appreciate
the growth of my faith and your incomprehensible
nature; and to know your peace which reigns in
me, yet surpasses my understanding. Thank you,
Jesus. Amen!

Week 7

Have I not commanded you? Be strong and courageous. Do not be frightened, and do not be dismayed, for the LORD your God is with you wherever you go.
Joshua 1:9

While your holy words tell me you are with me wherever I go, let me truly believe this. I always find you with me in the joyful times, but I wonder where you are when I am scared and troubled. Help me understand that this Scripture is not a mere pat on the head or a passive "I'll be there for you," but you give an actual command to stand firm and brave in times of trouble. You are my one true master, so I pray that I take your words to heart and act upon your decrees. In your name, I pray. Amen!

Week 8

∎ ∎ ∎

I wait for the LORD, my soul waits,
and in his word I hope.
Psalm 130:5

Father, let me not only pray to you but also take the time to read your word. Give me wisdom to comprehend the spiritual nature of your Scripture. These are not simple words put on the page by people but Spirit-led works of poetry, narrative, parables, and teachings, which give me hope— hope that allows me to live life more abundantly regardless of my circumstances and conditions. I give you thanks and praise for your holy Scripture. Amen!

Week 9

*Be alert, stand firm in the faith,
be brave, be strong. Do all your
work in love.*
1 Corinthians 16:13-14 (GNT)

I pray for the work I do, Lord. Whether it be performing the rituals of laundry, lawn work, spreadsheets, or special projects, may I approach each task with love. A love that pours with desire from my very heart to give you glory and spread your gospel. Be my cornerstone so that I may indeed have the courage and strength to advance your kingdom in all I do. Be with me, oh Lord, in all that I do. Amen!

Week 10

He has shown you, O mortal, what is good.
And what does the LORD require of you?
To act justly and to love mercy and to walk
humbly with your God.
Micah 6:8 (NIV)

Lord, open my heart so I may understand your definition of justice, mercy, and humility. I do not want to define these things as the world defines them, but as your holy Scripture explains them to me. Allow me to comprehend how you would have me act, love, and walk as I imitate you, Christ, every day. I know all of this comes through your commandment to love others as you loved me. Thank you, Jesus. Amen!

Week 11

I have been crucified with Christ. It is no longer I who live, but Christ who lives in me. And the life I now live in the flesh I live by faith in the Son of God, who loved me and gave himself for me.
Galatians 2:20

Dear Jesus, how can I live in my flesh and still honor you? I cannot bear the thought of you being crucified for my sins, let alone think of myself suffering as you did. I could never have done what you did for me and this world. You, however, served as the one great sacrifice. In your crucifixion, all sin died and was buried as you rose again, showing us that death and sin have no hold on us any longer. My sin was put to death in you, and now I live, even in my flesh. I have faith and acceptance of Christ as my Savior. I am loved. I thank you for your mercy and grace given to me and to all who will accept you. I give you thanks and pray in your name. Amen!

Week 12

*It will be said on that day,
"Behold, this is our God; we have waited
for him, that he might save us. This is the
LORD; we have waited for him; let us be
glad and rejoice in his salvation."
Isaiah 25:9*

Father, it is so difficult to wait. I want things now. Yet, when I read this verse from Isaiah, I cannot begin to comprehend the impatience, frustration, and longing the people of Israel felt as they waited for their Messiah. I get to know you here and now. The waiting is over. To you, I give thanks and praise for what you have done for me. I rejoice in the salvation you have given me through your death and resurrection. Forgive me for my impatience. Allow me to be attuned to your will so that I may, in turn, be glad and rejoice in what you have in store for me, no matter your timeline. Praise be to you, Father. Amen!

Week 13

And the peace of God, which surpasses all understanding, will guard your hearts and your minds in Christ Jesus.
Philippians 4:7

Dear Father, so many times, my world seems out of control. In my loss, in my anger and frustration, and in my anxiety and fears, I find no comfort, only pain. Lift my heart, Lord, with a peace that I cannot understand. A peace that can only flow from you as my redeemer. Let me crawl up into your arms and rest, comforted by the heartbeat in your chest.

May this peace not only comfort me, but protect me from future valleys I will find myself in. Let my heart and mind be shielded from self-destroying thoughts and the negative words of others. You only bring goodness to me even in difficult times. Let me cling to this peace that sets me free. In your name, I pray. Amen!

Week 14

■ ■ ■

But I have prayed for you that your faith may not fail. And when you have turned again, strengthen your brothers.
Luke 22:32

I know my faith falters. Doubts seep into my heart and mind. Renew in me a deep faith so that I may trust in you even more than I do at this moment. May my hardened heart be softened and my mind be filled with your wisdom so that my faith may be alive. Within this renewal of faith, allow me to be a conduit for your words and love to others. Allow me to be a light in the darkness of this world. May my faith be a pillar of strength to others. I cannot do this on my own but only through your strength, love, and compassion. Thank you for all that you do for me. I pray in your name, Jesus. Amen!

Week 15

*For I know the plans and thoughts that
I have for you, says the LORD, plans for
peace and well-being and not for disaster,
to give you a future and a hope.
Jeremiah 29:11 (AMP)*

Oh, dear God, I cannot thank you enough for the blessings you give me each and every day. I secretly desire to know all the plans and thoughts you have for me. Yet, I know that having this wisdom would do me more harm than good. I would not be able to handle what you have in store for me. Let me not desire to know the future but to live in the present with you. I can have peace in understanding that my future is full of the hope found in you. Thank you, Jesus. Amen!

Week 16

Therefore, as you received Christ Jesus the Lord, so walk in him, rooted and built up in him and established in the faith, just as you were taught, abounding in thanksgiving.
Colossians 2:6-7

Lord, you are my Savior. Let me now live out what have you as my Savior entails. Allow me to be an example of you to others. Remind me that I can only draw closer to you by reading your words, praying, and listening for your voice. I thank you for those who have guided me on my journey with you—for the people who led me to you and to those who continue to lead me today. Above all, I give my life to you. May I be ever thankful for your grace and mercy, which you give freely to all, even me. I pray this in your name, Jesus. Amen!

Week 17

I will remember the deeds of the LORD;
yes, I will remember your wonders of old.
I will ponder all your work, and meditate
on your mighty deeds.
Psalm 77:11-12

Draw me closer to your word to read the Scripture as breathed from you, oh Father. Only in this intimacy can I understand all the works of your hands. To see the mighty deeds you have performed throughout all generations, from your creation to where I stand today. Your actions are woven into the story you have written about me. May I recall all that you have given and done for me throughout my life. When I rise, when I lay down, and all the hours in between, allow me to meditate on your wonderful deeds and how they have impacted my life and shaped my future. Thank you, Jesus. Amen!

Week 18

■ ■ ■

Do not use harmful words, but only helpful words, the kind that build up and provide what is needed, so that what you say will do good to those who hear you.
Ephesians 4:29 (GNT)

Jesus, may my lips be guarded. Do not allow words to escape that are negative toward others, or join in gossip, slander, or libel. May my words give life as you give life. Allow me to speak through the darkness within my own heart and be a light to others in my speech. Let me hold back in my cursing and instead give sound words of encouragement. Your words gave life and meaning to all who heard and still listen today. If my words can provide even a tenth of that wisdom to those around me, then let it be so. I pray this in your holy name. Amen!

Week 19

He must increase, but I must decrease.
John 3:30

Let this short verse build within me so I can truly master your call. That I may be a servant to you and to others. In my life, there needs to be more of you and less of me. In times of trouble, fear, frustration, anxiety, or whatever valley I am in, allow me to step aside and become less so you can become more in my life. In times of praise and great joy, remind me that I did not accomplish anything on my own but only as you allowed, understanding that having more of you in my life will bring me joy regardless of my circumstances. Thank you, Jesus. Amen!

Week 20

■ ■ ■

Yet this I call to mind and therefore I have hope: Because of the LORD's great love we are not consumed, for his compassions never fail. They are new every morning; great is your faithfulness.
Lamentations 3:21-23 (NIV)

Father, in the midst of my wandering from you and in my suffering, allow me to always be mindful of the hope found in you. May my heart and mind focus on your enduring love, which is with me and in me day and night. Even as I sleep, you heal me physically, emotionally, and spiritually so that I awake to a new day. May I look upon everything in the morning and see, grasp, and rejoice in your creation, understanding how great your faithfulness is to a sinner like me. In your sweet name, I pray, Jesus. Amen!

Week 21

And I will give you a new heart, and a new spirit I will put within you. And I will remove the heart of stone from your flesh and give you a heart of flesh.
Ezekiel 36:26

Teach me, God, to not only recognize my sin but also to understand how it hardens my heart toward you. I do not want to stray or become jaded against your presence, mercy, and grace. I desire my heart to beat for you, to understand my sin and bring it forth to you. Let me be cleansed by confessing my sins to you today. In my acceptance of you as my Savior, remove my hardened heart and replace it with a heart of love for you as the first and foremost person in my life. Jesus, I lift this prayer up to you. Amen!

Week 22

Likewise the Spirit helps us in our weakness. For we do not know what to pray for as we ought, but the Spirit himself intercedes for us with groanings too deep for words.
Romans 8:26

Thank you, God. I cannot praise you enough. Not only have you loved me to the point of allowing your own Son to die for me that I might live with you forever, but you have given us the Holy Spirit. The Spirit who knows us as intimately as you know me. The Spirit who cries out to you with prayers for my good. Even if I do not know what is best or have no way to express what is in my heart, your Spirit addresses you on my behalf. Thank you for this blessing. In your name, Jesus, I pray. Amen!

Week 23

* * *

Restore to me the joy of your salvation and grant me a willing spirit, to sustain me. Then I will teach transgressors your ways, so that sinners will turn back to you.
Psalm 51:12-13 (NIV)

Father, forgive me of my sins. I lay my heart bare before you. Please have mercy on me. As I experience your loving forgiveness, allow me to share this with others. We all fall short of your love, and yet, you forgive us, Jesus. Thank you for something that I am undeserving of. Give me the situations and the words to speak to others about your forgiveness and your love that can be experienced and to understand the freedom found in you. Thank you, Jesus. Amen!

Week 24

Then you will call upon me and come and pray to me, and I will hear you. You will seek me and find me, when you seek me with all your heart.
Jeremiah 29:12-13

I do pray to you, Father. Bring me into a right relationship with you. I want to shout to the world of your loving kindness so others can experience what I have in you. I am amazed that you hear a sinner such as myself. Thank you. Do not let me pray to you while distracted or treating our time as a simple "do this for me now, God." I want my whole heart devoted to you in prayer and at all times. I will look for you in the storms and the quiet of the morning and before I shut my eyes at night. To think this wholehearted approach to you will lead me to you and I will hear your voice. I pray this in your name, Jesus, as I listen for you. Amen!

Week 25

Rejoice in hope, be patient in tribulation, be constant in prayer.
Romans 12:12

I have to be constant in prayer, Lord, if I am to get through any day. I wrestle with so many things in my heart and mind. Some that disturb me and others in which I can delight with you. Thank you for allowing me to come to you with my fears, anxiety, and frustrations. Teach me patience, God, even though I'm scared to ask for that. However, I know deep inside that it is the hope I have in you that teaches me to be patient through my struggles. Thank you for the blessings you have given me. In your name, I pray, Jesus. Amen!

Week 26

■ ■ ■

*Now, Lord, consider their threats and
enable your servants to speak your word
with great boldness.
Acts 4:29 (NIV)*

Give me strength. Give me clarity of speech. Give
me discernment so I know when to speak and
when to stay quiet. Give me words that cut to the
core in the same loving way you spoke to people.
Do not let me be timid, but willing to shout your
saving message, the gospel, the good news, so that
all within my reach may hear. Let your words speak
through me. Let me be a conduit for your loving
grace and mercy. May my words be a sweet, sweet
sound to you and those around me. I ask this in
your name, Jesus. Amen!

Week 27

*Little children, let us not love in word or talk
but in deed and in truth.*
1 John 3:18

Oh, Father, let me sit at your feet and learn of your love. I want to understand how I can conduct myself in love and, through this love, shine your truth. As James wrote about the power of the tongue, let me not forget that I should not speak about love and at the same time curse others. Instead, love should be seen through my actions. Allow me to be your means through which the Spirit of truth shines through me so others may come to know you. May both my words and deeds reflect your love for all. In your sweet name, Jesus, I pray. Amen!

Week 28

But I have trusted in your steadfast love;
my heart shall rejoice in your salvation. I
will sing to the LORD, because he has dealt
bountifully with me.
Psalm 13:5-6

Dear Jesus, I praise you. Your love for me never changes. I have received salvation because you died for me, and I accept you as my Savior and the Lord of my life. How can I not but praise you and rejoice in the gift of life you gave to me? Regardless of the condition I find myself in, be it rich or poor, healthy or sick, in community or alone, I can and will praise you. The bountiful life you give comes not from this world but from your sacrifice. This is all the bounty I need. On this, let me be content. Praise you, Jesus. Amen!

Week 29

Remember that I have commanded you to be determined and confident! Do not be afraid or discouraged, for I, the LORD your God, am with you wherever you go.
Joshua 1:9 (GNT)

Father, I know these words you spoke to Joshua so long ago still ring true today. You are with me wherever I am. Let me feel the spark of the Holy Spirit within me at all times. Allow me to approach each day in confidence, knowing I am secure in you. You are the only security I need, for there is nothing in this world that provides everlasting love like you do. May I always call upon you in times of distress and discouragement so your strength and comfort can surround me.

Let me also recall your great commandment to love you with all my heart, soul, and mind and to love my neighbor as myself. Filled with this type of love, I can go forward confident that I am serving you and doing your will. Thank you, Jesus. Amen!

Week 30

*Though the fig tree should not blossom,
nor the fruit be on the vines, the produce
of the olive fail and the fields yield no food,
the flock be cut off from the fold and there
be no herd in the stalls, yet I will rejoice in
the LORD; I will take joy in the God of my
salvation.*
Habakkuk 3:17-18

Lord, be with me in all areas of life. Let me be content with the highs and lows of my life. May my mind always focus on your eternal view. Let me understand that the things of this world pale in comparison to what is to come. Even in times of need, I can take joy in the salvation you have offered me, and I have accepted. Do not let me forget you in times of discouragement, but always let me give you a thankful heart. Understanding your salvation cures all ills because this world will pass, and the new heaven and earth will be joy and peace, which I can only imagine. Thank you for your generosity. I give my life to you, Jesus. Amen!

Week 31

If we confess our sins, he is faithful and just to forgive us our sins and to cleanse us from all unrighteousness.
1 John 1:9

Forgive me, Father, for I have sinned. I rebel against you constantly, even when I try not to. I am filthy in your eyes, Father, and yet you gave your only Son whose death and resurrection cleanses me. My heart is hardened like coal against you at times, and yet, when I confess my sins, you change my heart into a diamond that reflects your love to all around me. I can never be perfect, but you, Jesus, can perfect me. For that, I am ever grateful.

I pray that you not only forgive me of my sins, but open my eyes so that I may begin to see my sin as it is and long to avoid it. Fill me with your Spirit to guard my heart and avoid my rebellious nature. Thank you for fighting for me in the spiritual realm so that I may fulfill your will for me. Thank you, Jesus, for your forgiveness. Amen!

Week 32

***

Be wise in the way you act toward outsiders; make the most of every opportunity. Let your conversation be always full of grace, seasoned with salt, so that you may know how to answer everyone.
Colossians 4:5-6 (NIV)

Touch my heart, oh God, and let me see people as you see them. I don't want to see the worst in people and walk away from them. Let me see and understand that they are your creation regardless of my opinion of them. May I approach all people, those I like and those I don't, and speak your truth to them. Let me speak your truth as you would speak it so that I know my conversations will always be full of grace. Do not let me condemn with my words, but lift up those I speak of, even in difficult conversations. Spirit, speak through me so that I will always have an answer for my faith, and wisely choose the words I speak to others. I pray in your name, Jesus. Amen!

Week 33

It is the LORD who goes before you. He will be with you; he will not leave you or forsake you. Do not fear or be dismayed.
Deuteronomy 31:8

Father, guard my heart from the fear and anxiety that live within me. Let me be confident that you are always with me. When I doubt, let me be still and focus on the truth that you are the great I Am. Not only do you walk with me, but you go before me to know what lies ahead. May I listen in my quiet time and deep within my soul to your presence and find the comfort you provide. Even Christ upon the cross spoke out and asked why you had forsaken him. So, give me the wisdom to understand that he spoke these words as one who took on all the sins of man, and I know I will never have to feel forsaken, for I am no longer separated from you. In all areas of my life may I feel your presence. Jesus, I pray this in your name. Amen!

Week 34

But Peter and John answered them, "Whether it is right in the sight of God to listen to you rather than to God, you must judge, for we cannot but speak of what we have seen and heard."
Acts 4:19-20

Lord, I pray that I have the courage of Peter and John. May I be so compelled by my knowledge of you that I can only speak of who you are. I ask that all words that leave my mouth glorify you. Allow the Holy Spirit to drive my words. May I speak the true gospel to those who are seeking you and lift up fellow believers so they may draw closer to you.

Let me also be courageous to speak of you even when the enemy is trying to silence your words. This may be through my own reticence or through outside pressures, but regardless, let me stand strong in faith and speak your words so that all can hear. Amen!

Week 35

First of all, then, I urge that supplications,
prayers, intercessions, and thanksgivings
be made for all people, for kings and all
who are in high positions, that we may
lead a peaceful and quiet life, godly and
dignified in every way.
1 Timothy 2:1-2

Oh, Father in heaven, do not let my mind or heart be poisoned by my attitudes and judgments toward others. Instead, allow me to lift up all people in prayer, including those I disagree with. I know we will not experience true peace until you come back again, but in the meantime, I pray for the leaders of my community, city, state, nation, and those across the globe so we may live peacefully.

Lord, you know the needs of others. I pray now that you would see fit to shine your light on their lives. I ask that you heal those who are suffering physically, emotionally, or spiritually. May they feel the comfort of your arms around them. For those that do not yet know you, soften their hearts so they may listen for you. Appear to them in dreams, visions, or in whatever way you may choose to communicate your love to them. Thank you for taking the time to listen to my prayers. In your name, Jesus, I pray. Amen!

Week 36

*Let me hear in the morning of your
steadfast love, for in you I trust.
Make me know the way I should go,
for to you I lift up my soul.
Psalm 143:8*

Thank you, Jesus, that I know I can trust in you.
When I open my eyes each morning and before
rising from bed, let me think first of you. Because of
your love for your creation, I know each morning
is a new day, which may or may not be my best day.
Allow me to see the day knowing that you guide
my footsteps regardless of my plans. As a deer
pants for water, so my soul longs after you. Jesus,
I lift up my soul to you, asking for every blessing
today so that I may first and foremost be your light
to others around me. Amen!

Week 37

*Now faith is confidence in what we
hope for and assurance about
what we do not see
Hebrews 11:1 (NIV)*

Father, renew my faith each and every day. May I find ways to draw closer to you. Let me recognize this blessed assurance of what I cannot see but know in my heart of hearts that you exist, you love, you comfort, you create, you strengthen, and you are the Alpha and Omega. Let me understand what it truly means to put my hope in you. To see you as my rock and cornerstone of my life. Strengthen me so that I may speak your word and be an active example of who you are and what you can do for those who follow you. I pray these things in your name. Amen!

Week 38

Why are you cast down, O my soul,
and why are you in turmoil within me?
Hope in God; for I shall again praise him,
my salvation and my God.
Psalm 42:11

Lord, there are days in which I feel that I have hit rock bottom in at least one area or all areas of my life. I struggle not only with the anxiety and depression of feeling this way, but I wonder how my spirit can be so downtrodden when I know that in you, I am saved. Joy is available with every breath I take.

Let me take this time in prayer and breathe in the very breath of God. May my soul be renewed. Even in the valleys I find myself in, may I turn and sing praises to you. Please let my words be a sweet, sweet sound to your ears. You alone are my salvation. Praise you, Jesus. In your name, I pray. Amen!

Week 39

*But seek first the kingdom of God
and his righteousness, and all these
things will be added to you.
Matthew 6:33*

What things will be added to me, Lord? What blessings will I find that you have in store for me? Father, I ask these questions because I want to know what you have in store for me, but I also know it is not for me to know. Teach me to seek your kingdom first, above all other things. To be content with what you have given me no matter how small or large. Let me seek your righteousness here on earth. Allow me to be satisfied with the minimum I need. Earlier in Matthew 6, Jesus talked about having nothing to worry about because our Father dresses the flowers and feeds the birds and how much more he will do for us. Again, I pray that I may fix all my heart and mind on the eternal life I have in you so none of this world matters anymore. Let me be diligent in serving you and finding your kingdom and righteousness. I pray in your name, sweet Jesus. Amen!

Week 40

***

Let no one despise you for your youth, but set the believers an example in speech, in conduct, in love, in faith, in purity.
1 Timothy 4:12

Allow me, Father, to be an example to others of your love. Guard my tongue so I only speak to build others up and not tear them down. Let me conduct myself in such a way that this world sees me as set apart and, thus, desires to know more about why I am different. Allow me to love others sacrificially as you loved me. May my faith in the unseen be strengthened by your spirit in me. A faith in you, Jesus, that is apparent to everyone. Give me a pure heart so that no negativity may be seen in me, and forgive me for those times when I rebel against the pure heart you have placed within me. Thank you for your grace and mercy, dear Father. Jesus, I pray all of this in your name. Amen!

Week 41

You are my hiding place and my shield;
I hope in your word.
Psalm 119:114

I pray, Father, that when life has me down, I hide in you and not in worldly desires that give me a brief escape from my troubles. You are everlasting and serve as a solid shelter against the enemy. I picture the Spartan soldiers who would gather in formation with their shields all around so they could continue to advance without being wounded by arrows. May your shield guard me as such. Please, Lord, shield my heart so that I do not go astray in times of plenty or when I have nothing. You, Jesus, are my stronghold.

Allow me to meditate on your word day and night so that I come to know you better. May I not only go through my laundry list of prayers but may I also take time to listen to you in my prayers and see your work in your word, knowing that your word applies to me just as it did in ancient days. I pray this all in your loving name. Amen!

Week 42

The LORD is my shepherd; I shall not want.
He makes me lie down in green pastures.
He leads me beside still waters.
Psalm 23:1-2

Lord, allow me to appreciate the beauty around me, such as the green grass and calming waters. I must confess, I bristle sometimes when I read that you will make me lie down. However, as my shepherd, my good shepherd, I must submit to you as you know best for me. Let me understand that what you make me do is in my own best interest. Thank you for caring for me so much that you know I need time to rest.

I thank you for providing for me. Let me be content with what you have given me. You give generously. Allow me to still believe in your generosity on the days I want more and am not satisfied. I also ask that you make me willing to take the excess I have and give it away generously. You have filled my cup so that it overflows, and I can never thank you enough for that. May I rest in the peace you provide for me. In your name, Jesus. Amen!

Week 43

LORD, I have given up my pride and turned away from my arrogance. I am not concerned with great matters or with subjects too difficult for me. Instead, I am content and at peace. As a child lies quietly in its mother's arms, so my heart is quiet within me.
Psalm 131:1-2 (GNT)

Father, let me find contentment and peace within my relationship with you. May I be content but not complacent. I always want to strive to be the person you want me to be. One who follows your will. One who loves you with all my soul, mind, and strength and who loves others as you love me.

Let me walk humbly with you, knowing that everything I have comes from you so that I may not boast about what I have completed but what you have done through me. Do not let me get caught up in arguments or discussions that do not lift you up or others. Never let me forget that I do not need to have all the answers but that my life is complete in you. Jesus, you have given me an eternal view so that I do not need to have full knowledge of the things of this world, but all I need is the faith of a child to understand what you require of me. I pray all these things in your name, Jesus. Amen!

Week 44

■ ■ ■

For all that is in the world – the desires of the flesh and the desires of the eyes and pride of life – is not from the Father but is from the world. And the world is passing away along with its desires, but whoever does the will of God abides forever
1 John 2:16-17

Lord, forgive me of my sins. Too often, I give in to the temptations of this world. I falter and need your forgiveness. I thank you that not only can I bring my sins before you, but I know as I lay them at the cross, I can walk away cleansed by your blood.

I wait with great anticipation for when a new heaven and earth will replace this fallen world, when all will be made new. Thank you for your sacrifice and for conquering death so that I may live forever. I know I am saved because I have invited you to be my Lord and Savior. Please allow me to understand your will for me. May I come to know you better and be attuned to your will by listening to you in my prayers and reading Scripture. Thank you. Amen!

Week 45

You, LORD, give perfect peace to those
who keep their purpose firm and
put their trust in you.
Isaiah 26:3 (GNT)

Please, Lord, grant me your peace. May I find joy in all situations, a joy that can only come from having peace that surpasses all understanding. Do not allow me to dwell on past mistakes, fears, arrogance, or other areas of my life that can sap my strength and cause me to falter. Instead, may I follow the path you have set before me with confidence and courage, knowing that you are with me throughout every day of my life. Let me trust in you with a trust that knows no end. Speak to me so that I may understand whatever comes my way and have confidence that I can trust you in all circumstances. I ask this of you, Jesus. Amen!

Week 46

■ ■ ■

And it is my prayer that your love may abound more and more, with knowledge and all discernment, so that you may approve what is excellent, and so be pure and blameless for the day of Christ.
Philippians 1:9-10

Father, I know that the apostle Paul wrote this to the church of Philippi, but I pray this for my family. May we abound in love—first and foremost with you and then with each other. May it be a love that is faithful, patient, and kind. A love that others can see in me and in my family. A love that keeps us on the straight and narrow path to your door, where you will answer and welcome us in. I look forward to the day that I may gaze upon your face and be forever comforted by your love for me, my family, and all who call you Savior. In your name, I pray. Amen!

Week 47

*Whatever you do, work heartily,
as for the Lord and not for men, knowing
that from the Lord you will receive
the inheritance as your reward.
You are serving the Lord Christ.
Colossians 3:23-24*

Please, Father, let me work for you. Let everything I do glorify you. May the works of my hands be an example of all the beauty you create. Do not allow me to get caught up in pride and arrogance over a job well done or a compliment from my manager, thinking I did this all by myself.

Jesus, I'm blown away as I think about how I will serve you when you come to seek and save the lost. You served as the ultimate sacrifice by giving your life, feeling the separation from your Father, and ultimately rising again to conquer death. So, I need not fear. Let me serve you well. Let me be your light in the wilderness when it is night and the dark is upon us. Allow me to reflect your love, kindness, and patience so that all can see you are the way, the truth, and the life. In your name, Jesus, I pray. Amen!

Week 48

*And let us not grow weary of
doing good, for in due season
we will reap, if we do not give up.
Galatians 6:9*

I must confess, Lord, that I grow weary. To be honest, I may not be weary, but simply want to have time for myself. Please give me discernment so I can understand the difference between a holy rest and simply being a sloth. This weighs heavily on my heart at times. Yet, I so want to do good for you. Jesus, you have done so much for me, and I didn't ask for it. The joy you instill in my heart leads me to desire to help others, to love others as myself, as you commanded.

Do not allow me to give up even when I struggle. May I always remember that in the good and difficult times, you are beside me. You, Jesus, walk by my side through the difficult times. This, too, causes me to sing praises to you and thank you for all the blessings I have. In your name, I lift these things up to you. Amen!

Week 49

*Create in me a pure heart, O God, and
renew a steadfast spirit within me.
Psalm 51:10 (NIV)*

Father, I am a sinful man, and I pray deeply that
you grant me your forgiveness. By your blood,
Jesus, I am made whole. My heart is no longer a
dark abyss but is now a shining light of your glory.
I can never thank you enough for this. I know that
you died for me and all of humanity so that we may
see you face-to-face one day and live forever in the
house of the Lord. I can think of nothing better or
that can even come close to the profound joy of
being forever in your presence. Praise you, Father,
Jesus, and Holy Spirit.

May my spirit always focus on you. Grant me
wisdom and discernment to understand not only
your words but also your actions. May I be ever
faithful to you as you are to me. Your love endures
forever. Thanks be to God. Amen!

Week 50

■ ■ ■

Put on then, as God's chosen ones, holy and beloved, compassionate hearts, kindness, humility, meekness, and patience.
Colossians 3:12

Father, allow me always to remember that not only do I need to put on my spiritual armor, but I also need to wear my compassionate heart, kindness, humility, meekness, and patience for all the world to see through my daily actions. Let me have compassion and not judge. Let me be kind and not bring others down with my words. Let me be humble and not tout my accomplishments to rise above others. Let me be meek so that I might endure my struggles with patience and without resentment. Let me be patient, understanding my life story happens in your perfect timing and not in my "satisfy me now" approach to life. In your name, I pray, Jesus. Amen!

Week 51

I have stored up your word in my heart,
that I might not sin against you.
Psalm 119:11

Allow me, Lord, to breathe in your Scripture that I may meditate on it day and night, as David exclaimed. Let your word live in me so that I may hold tight to it as I praise you and hide in you during the rough times in my life. Let your word be an inoculation against my sinful life. Let every thought I have be taken captive and turned over to you to keep or throw out. I want to focus on you, Jesus. Allow me to use your word to tell everyone about you. You are my Lord and Savior. Let me not use your word to hurt others but to build them up. Let me be so mindful that anything I quote from the Bible is aligned with your will. You are a great and wonderful God who has given us heavenly Scripture to build our lives upon and to grow in trusting you. I pray in your name. Amen!

Week 52

■ ■ ■

In the same way, let your light shine before others, so that they may see your good works and give glory to your Father who is in heaven.
Matthew 5:16

Jesus, let me be your light here on earth. May I simply reflect your love, goodness, and holiness to others. Let the good things I do be celebrated as works of your hand, not of my own. Jesus, let me look upon this Scripture as a command from you so that I take it to heart and live it and breathe it every day. Let your will be done and not mine, for I would simply complicate matters and make them all about me. But I must understand that the good I do is out of love for you. I want to please you through my faith in you, which is worked out by my actions.

All glory and honor be to you, oh God. I look forward to the day that I will praise you 24/7 in your presence. I cannot begin to fathom the joy that will explode from me when this day comes. You are holy indeed. Thanks and praise be to you, God. I lift these words to you and ask for your blessing. Amen!